D0906972

YOU HAVE A PET WHAT?!

SKUNK

Ann Matzke

Rourke
Educational Media

rourkeeducationalmedia.com

Before & After Reading Activities

Before Reading:

Building Academic Vocabulary and Background Knowledge

Before reading a book, it is important to tap into what your child or students already know about the topic. This will help them develop their vocabulary, increase their reading comprehension, and make connections across the curriculum.

1. *Look at the cover of the book. What will this book be about?*
2. *What do you already know about the topic?*
3. *Let's study the Table of Contents. What will you learn about in the book's chapters?*
4. *What would you like to learn about this topic? Do you think you might learn about it from this book? Why or why not?*
5. *Use a reading journal to write about your knowledge of this topic. Record what you already know about the topic and what you hope to learn about the topic.*
6. *Read the book.*
7. *In your reading journal, record what you learned about the topic and your response to the book.*
8. *After reading the book complete the activities below.*

Content Area Vocabulary
Read the list. What do these words mean?

burrow
den
domesticated
glands
legal
litter
omnivores
rabies
warns

After Reading:

Comprehension and Extension Activity

After reading the book, work on the following questions with your child or students in order to check their level of reading comprehension and content mastery.

1. *Why is a pet skunk not the best choice for some families? (Summarize)*
2. *Why would someone want to keep skunks as pets? (Infer)*
3. *How are skunks similar to dogs and cats? (Asking questions)*
4. *How would caring for a pet change your daily life? (Text to self connection)*
5. *What is unique about a skunk's fur? (Asking questions)*

Extension Activity

Skunks are considered an exotic pet and need the special care of a trained veterinarian. Ask an adult to help you contact a veterinarian who cares for exotic pets. Develop questions and interview them about caring for exotic pets. Gather unique facts about each one. Make a poster and include pictures of the different exotic animals and unique facts. Share your poster with your classmates and friends.

Table of Contents

Little Stinkers

When you think of skunks do you think, *Pee-yew!*? A skunk's reputation as a natural stinker **warns** us to stay away. But remove their bad smell, and this boldly striped animal is curious, quick to learn, and tenderhearted.

For some people, skunks make great pets. They can live indoors with humans just like cats and dogs.

Pet Pointers

A pet skunk's musky scent **glands** can be removed when it is about four weeks old.

Close in size to a cat or small dog, skunks weigh about 11 pounds (5 kilograms).

Wild skunks live in North America from Mexico to Canada. There are different types and colors of skunks.

The black-and-white striped skunk found in parts of North America is a member of the mephitis mephitis *animal family.*

Domesticated black and white striped skunks are now bred as pets.

Skunks: Head to Toe

eyes ❯

fur ⌄

paws ❯

legs ❯

Eyes

The skunk doesn't have great eyesight. It can't see objects more than about 10 feet (3 meters) away.

Fur

A skunk's fur has two layers. The short, curly fur next to their skin keeps them warm. The longer, shiny fur keeps them dry.

Legs

Skunks have stubby legs. They waddle when they walk, but if frightened they can run short distances.

Musk Glands

Under a skunk's tail are two small glands that store the strong-smelling oil. The ends of the glands are like hoses. The skunk will spray the stinky oil when it senses danger.

Paws

A skunk has long, curved claws in front. These claws are important for handling food and digging. The back claws are shorter.

Tail

The skunk's tail is long and bushy. It will raise its tail as a warning.

‹ musk glands

‹ tail

Baby Skunks

A group of skunks is called a surfeit. Babies are called kits. A mother skunk gives birth to a **litter** of five or seven kits at a time.

At birth, a skunk's eyes are closed. They have almost no fur, but a black and white pattern can be seen on their pink skin.

Want to Own a Pet Skunk?

Pet skunks are **legal** in 17 states. Each state may have different rules, though. Check with your state's authorities before you buy.

Ask your breeder for a health certificate. Save your receipt of payment to prove your skunk was purchased and not from the wild.

Check this map to see if owning a skunk is legal in your state:

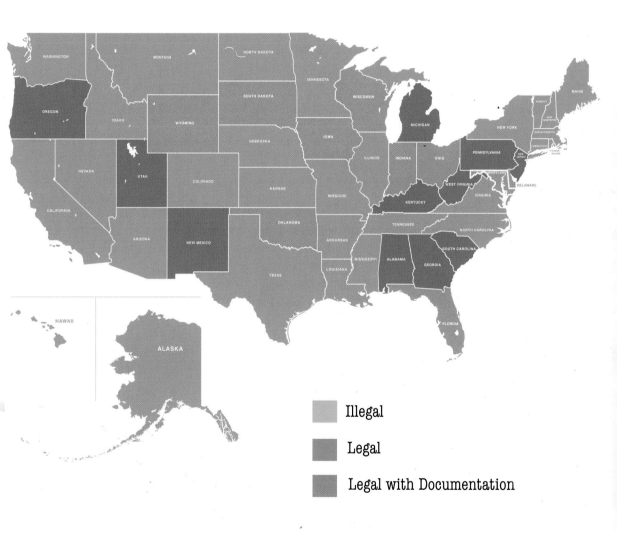

Illegal

Legal

Legal with Documentation

Skunks like to **burrow** and will set up their **den** in a quiet, dark place like a cabinet or a large box. They will build a nest from old towels, blankets or clothing. If you leave things lying around, they might take it for their den!

FUN FACT

Skunks are nocturnal in the wild but a pet skunk will adapt to your awake and sleep schedule.

Handle your skunk right away. Use your hands for holding and cuddling. Play gently.

Pet Pointers

To avoid a skunk's sharp teeth, use a stuffed animal or a puppet at playtime.

The more you hold, cuddle, and talk to your new skunk the more you are encouraging them to be calm and lovable. Touching their feet, paws, and mouth will help with feeding and trimming claws as they grow older.

Skunks, like any pet, need discipline. It is difficult for skunks to know when they are playing or biting too hard. Never hit or spank. Use the tone and volume of your voice to correct a wrong behavior. Help them understand by using a time-out system to remove them from the situation.

Pet Pointers

Skunks have excellent memories. They never forget being mistreated, and rarely forgive.

Place your pet skunk in a time-out container they can't crawl out of for a few minutes. Stay nearby.

Skunks are **omnivores**. They eat plants and meat. A skunk's daily diet should be made up of about 40 percent fruits and vegetables, and 60 percent meat and dairy.

Skunks have big appetites and may overeat. Discuss a balanced diet and feeding schedule with a veterinarian to prevent obesity.

Litter Training

Skunks are quite clean and will choose a corner to use as a bathroom. Accept their choice and place several layers of newspaper or an open litter pan with cat litter, wood pellets, or recycled paper. Keep the corner clean or they'll choose a different corner.

Keeping your Skunk Healthy and Safe

Be choosy about a veterinarian. Find one that cares for skunks. Be informed about your skunk's health. Vaccinations are required. All skunks have roundworms and must be treated.

Talk to your veterinarian about removing musk glands and being spayed or neutered. This will help prevent behavior problems later.

Pet Pointers

Skunks will dig where they smell something to eat. They can be destructive, pulling up carpet, digging into wallboard, and scratching at closed doors.

A pet skunk is like having a younger brother or sister. Their natural curiosity can lead to danger. Once they know how to do something, they will do it again and again.

Skunk-proof your house: Add safety latches on cabinets. Block the space behind washers and dryers, and refrigerators. Secure vents and windows. Place wastebaskets in secure areas. Remove poisonous products. Be watchful of electric cords and outlets. Never leave windows open.

Skunks don't like water, but can swim if necessary. They do not need a regular bath, but can smell musky at times.

Domesticated pet skunks do not carry the **rabies** virus. A skunk must be bitten by another animal sick with the rabies virus to become infected. If you have questions, talk to your veterinarian. Consider vaccinating against rabies and know the laws about reporting skunk bites.

Skunk Talk

Skunks are sensitive animals, full of emotion. They like to communicate their feelings.

Here are some ways skunks communicate:
Happy: smack their lips
Wanting attention: chirp like a bird
Mad: squeal or whine
Sad or frightened: whimper like a dog
Upset: grumble, grunt, or stomp their feet

When skunks are playing it might look like they are dancing. They'll run forward, stop, stomp their paws, back up, swoosh their tails, and spin around.

Playing is just the beginning of the fun you can have with a pet skunk. Spend time loving and caring for these unique animals and they will love you back.

Things to Think About
If You Want a Pet Skunk

- Is it legal to keep a skunk where you live?
- A skunk can live up to ten years. Will you be able to care for it its whole life?
- Do you have a local experienced veterinarian who treats skunks?
- If you have other pets, how will they interact with a skunk?
- Is your home secure enough that your pet won't escape? A skunk can travel several miles a day if it gets loose.
- Pet skunks require a lot of specialized care. Is your family ready to make the commitment?

Glossary

burrow (BUR-oh): a tunnel or hole in the ground made or used by a rabbit, or other animal, such as a skunk

den (den): the home of a wild animal, such as a lion

domesticated (duh-MESS-tuh-kate-ud): something tamed so it can live with or be used by human beings

glands (glands): organs in the body that either produces natural chemicals or allows substances to leave the body, as in sweat glands

legal (LEE-guhl): lawful, or allowed by law

litter (LIT-ur): a group of animals born at the same time to one mother

omnivores (OM-nuh-vorz): animals that eat both plants and meat

rabies (RAY-beez): an often fatal disease that can affect humans, dogs, bats and other warm-blooded animals. Rabies is caused by a virus that attacks the brain and spinal cord and is spread by the bite of an infected animal

warns (worns): tells someone about a danger or a bad thing that might happen

Index

Show What You Know

1. Are skunks legal in your state?

2. What do skunks eat?

3. How do skunks communicate?

4. List three ways to keep your skunk safe.

5. What is the best way to play with a skunk?

Websites to Visit

www.justskunks.com

www.skunkhaven.net/StatesForm.htm

www.skunk-info.org

About the Author

Ann H. Matzke has an MFA in writing for children and young adults from Hamline University. She grew up loving animals and had many different kinds of pets: cats, fish, turtles, hamsters, gerbils and even fire-bellied toads. Ann and her family live in Gothenburg, Nebraska, with their Labradors, Penny and Lucy, and three cats, Max, Michael, and Foggy Nelson. Ann enjoys traveling, reading, and photography.

Meet The Author!
www.meetREMauthors.com

PHOTO CREDITS: Cover, pg 4, 5, 17: ©Alona Rjabeca; page 1: ©twphotos; page 3: ©sbrogan; page 6: ©karlumbriaco; page 8-9, 22, 26: ©GlobalP; page 11: ©aatuna; page 14: ©Eric Isselé; page 15: ©Becky Sheridan; page 16: ©Silvia Boratti; page 18: ©Teerpun; page 19: ©stickytoffeepudding; page 20: ©monkeybusinessimages; page 21: ©michaeljung; page 23: ©michalbryc; page 24: ©ShelleyPerry; page 25: ©Teka77; page 27: ©Snowshill; page 28: ©Nathan0834; page 29: ©Brainsil

Edited by: Keli Sipperley
Cover and interior design by: Rhea Magaro-Wallace

Library of Congress PCN Data

Skunk / Ann Matzke
(You Have a Pet What?!)
ISBN 978-1-68342-179-5 (hard cover)
ISBN 978-1-63432-245-7 (e-Book)
Library of Congress Control Number: 2016956601

Printed in the United States of America, North Mankato, Minnesota

Also Available as:

ROURKE'S
e-Books